JAMES ROBERT

DANGERS IN OBSESSIVE LOVE DISORDER

Table of content

Chapter 5-Treatment on obsessive love disorder

Introduction

Obsessive love disorder is described by huge degrees of doubt in memory (for example for activities). Amusingly, this brought down certainty is to some degree to a limited extent because of continued checking, which is expected to bring down perceptual handling and subsequently decreases striking quality and detail of the memories. In a past report. Reality checking and metacognitive convictions connected with mental trust in saw that OLD isn't just described by decreased trust in memory, yet in addition by a comparable doubt in consideration. The current review pointed toward repeating and expanding this finding. It was seen that patients experiencing OLD showed less trust in consideration and memory than a clinical and a nonclinical control bunch, that trust in consideration was extraordinarily connected with really taking a look at conduct, and that continued actually taking a look at caused expanded degrees of doubt in consideration. Furthermore, it was seen that mental doubt while performing OLD-related activities reaches out to consideration, yet additionally to insight. It is contended that examination on metacognition in OLD ought to move past the investigation of memory.

CHAPTER 1

WHAT IS OBSESSIVE LOVE:

Love can be an euphoric inclination, yet many individuals have felt the torment of a messed up heart and the force of captivation. Obsessive love takes these feelings further, making an individual focus on their cherished one like they are an item or ownership.

Wellbeing experts don't broadly perceive obsessive love, or over the top love issue, as an emotional well-being condition.

For sure, it isn't right now recorded in the Demonstrative and Factual Manual of Mental Issues in any case, over the top love can be an indication of other psychological well-being difficulties and conditions.

On the off chance that the individual encountering sensations of obsessive love doesn't get treatment for the general side effects, they might experience issues controlling these sentiments. In exceptionally outrageous cases, this might significantly set off an individual to carry out demonstrations of viciousness or misuse.

This article talks about obsessive love, the causes and side effects behind it, and some conceivable treatment choices.

Love can likewise cause actual changes in the body and may include:

chemicals like oxytocin, vasopressin, cortisol, and testosterone

synapses like dopamine and serotonin

nerve development factor

For certain individuals, these sentiments might be strong to the point that they become fixated on keeping and controlling the individual they love.

They might seem to love their accomplice on occasion, however become upset or desirous at the smallest danger.

fascination

reverberation or association

trust

regard

A portion of these elements might be absent in obsessive love. For instance, individuals with outrageous desire may not believe their accomplice which might prompt them attempting to control their accomplice or continually checking their way of behaving.

Obsessive love might zero in on responsibility for accomplice, as opposed to considering them to be an equivalent. Instead of adoring the individual and needing the best for them, individuals with over the top propensities might cherish the other individual in view of their own requirements.

Relationship obsessive enthusiastic problem incorporates fixations on a nearby or close connection or accomplice and may remember an over the top concentration for how an accomplice is temperamental or deceitful. Obsessive doubt in a relationship might connection to wretchedness, nervousness, and brutality in a relationship.

Obsessive love may at times include a relationship that

doesn't really exist, for example, with a big name or an outsider.

Erotomania is a mental problem wherein an individual has a hallucinating beliefTrusted Source that an individual of higher societal position than them is infatuated with them. With erotomania, the attention is on getting love, instead of giving affection.

CHAPTER 2

WHAT IS OBSESSIVE LOVE DISORDER:

Obsessive love disorder is a condition that makes you experience over the top sentiments you could confuse as adoration with someone else. An individual with obsessive love disorder will enjoy these sentiments, in any case on the off chance that they are responded or not. Love is a recognizable feeling for a great many people. We have affection toward our pets, companions, and family. At the point when sensations of adoration or seemingly love for an individual are joined by an obsession or a craving to control someone else, this could be obsessive love disorder.

Obsessive love disorder isn't presently named an emotional well-being condition. This is on the grounds that there has been some discussion about whether over the top love problem can be viewed as an emotional well-being condition.

obsessive love disorder , a genuine crippling condition could impede one's everyday working whenever left untreated. It could likewise make them have useless associations with individuals they are enamored with.

In a few outrageous cases, it could likewise represent a danger to the object of an individual's obsession, particularly when sentiments are not responded.

CHAPTER 3

CAUSES OF OBSESSIVE LOVE DISORDER:

Love Disorder to other, all the more well realized psychological wellness issues, it tends to be trying to analyze. Likewise, side effects might shift for various individuals.

Since obsessive love disorder isn't delegated a psychological well-being condition, it is difficult for it to have a recognizable reason. Be that as it may, it has been connected to other emotional well-being disorder, for example, post-horrendous pressure problem, fanatical enthusiastic issue, and marginal behavioral condition

Overpowering fascination with one individual

Possessive contemplations and activities

Extraordinary distraction with a relationship

Undermining the other individual assuming they leave

Outrageous envy

Continued informing through message, email, or calls

Observing the other individual's activities

Powerlessness to endure time away for an individual

Obscuring or crossing limits

Tension

Becoming hopelessly enamored rapidly with new colleagues

Controlling way of behaving

Relational disorder have been generally emphatically connected to setting obsessive love disorder. At the point when an individual can't shape sound connections with others, this influences the nature of connections they have and how they act with others.

For certain individuals with an emotional issues, the condition could cause them to feel far off from potential or current accomplices. For other people, an emotional issues can make them become over the top with individuals they structure an association with.

CHAPTER 4

Difference between love and obsession:

1: Aim

The distinction among adoration and fixation begins with what's the point of the relationship. Individuals who go into connections to feel much better about themselves and make up for a shortfall are bound to wind up fixating on somebody.

On the other hand, solid connections have areas of strength for an of help for both. Many off track love tunes guarantee they can't survive without somebody or even inhale without them. That is fixation, not love.

2: Limits

Take a gander at the time you spend all together for how to be aware in the event that you're fixated on somebody. Solid love values the two individuals as people while additionally guaranteeing the requirements of the couple. Limits are significant so you can act naturally. Like that, your accomplice perceives the truth about you and not as they wish you were.

On the off chance that, on the other side, you're joined at the hip without time alone for yourself or your companions, you could be managing the signs somebody is fixated on you. Hold perusing to the following segment to decide whether it's you, your accomplice or a touch of both.

3: Feelings

A portion of the conspicuous signs

somebody is fixated on you are the explosions of feelings. These could be anything from desire to possessiveness and control. An unfortunate fixation on an individual prompts uneasiness and stress which by and large weakens feelings.

4: Nonsensical versus grounded conduct

What causes a fixation on an individual is connected to some type of injury or mental irregularity. Considering this, it's not shocking that the signs somebody is fixated on you include unpredictable way of behaving.

This could incorporate faulting you for cheating since you get back home from work late. You could likewise wind up legitimizing why you're calling sure companions. Add to that, close to home fits and you'll get the signs somebody is fixated on you.

5: Reason

Watch others for how to be aware on the off chance that you're fixated on somebody.

Basically, stable couples effectively continue on from the fascination stage since they fabricate their relationship on a strong groundwork. Normal qualities are significant just like the general reason to stay away from the indications of fanatical pondering somebody.

CHAPTER 5

TREATMENT ON OBSESSIVE LOVE DISORDER:

Moves toward assist with treating over the top love problem might include:

Mental assessment. This incorporates talking about your viewpoints, sentiments, side effects and ways of behaving to decide whether you have fixations or impulsive ways of behaving that impede your personal satisfaction. With your consent, this might incorporate conversing with your family or companions.

Analytic measures for OCD. Your PCP might involve measures in the

Demonstrative and Factual Manual of Mental Problems. This might be finished to assist with precluding different issues that could be causing your side effects and to check for any connected complexities.

Picking a medicine. As a rule, the objective is to control side effects at the most minimal conceivable dose successfully.

Attempting a few medications prior to finding one that functions admirably is entirely normal. Your primary care physician could prescribe more than one drug to deal with your side effects actually. It can require a long time to months subsequent to beginning a medicine to see an improvement in side effects.

Incidental effects. All mental drugs make possible side impacts.

Converse with your primary care physician about conceivable secondary effects and about any wellbeing observing required while ingesting mental medications. Also, let your PCP know as to whether you experience alarming incidental effects.

Self destruction risk. Most antidepressants are by and large protected, expects that all antidepressants convey black box admonitions, the strictest alerts for remedies. At times, kids, teens and youthful grown-ups under 25 might have an expansion in self-destructive contemplations or conduct while taking antidepressants, particularly in the initial not many weeks in the wake of beginning or when the portion is changed. Assuming self-destructive contemplations happen, promptly contact your PCP or get crisis help. Remember that antidepressants are bound to diminish self destruction risk over the long haul by further developing temperament.

Cooperations with different substances. While taking an energizer, educate your PCP concerning some other remedy or non-prescription meds, spices or different enhancements you take.

A few antidepressants can make a few different meds less viable and cause perilous responses when joined with specific drugs or home grown supplements.

Halting antidepressants. Antidepressants aren't viewed as habit-forming, however once in a while actual reliance (which is unique in relation to fixation) can happen. So halting treatment unexpectedly or missing a few dosages can cause withdrawal-like side effects, some of the time called stopping disorder. Try not to quit taking your drug without conversing with your primary care physician, regardless of whether you're feeling improved — you might have a backslide of OCD side effects. Work with your PCP to step by step and securely decline your portion.

www.ingramcontent.com/pod-product-compliance
Lightning Source LLC
LaVergne TN
LVHW080817170826
845678LV00011B/2050

9798362748876